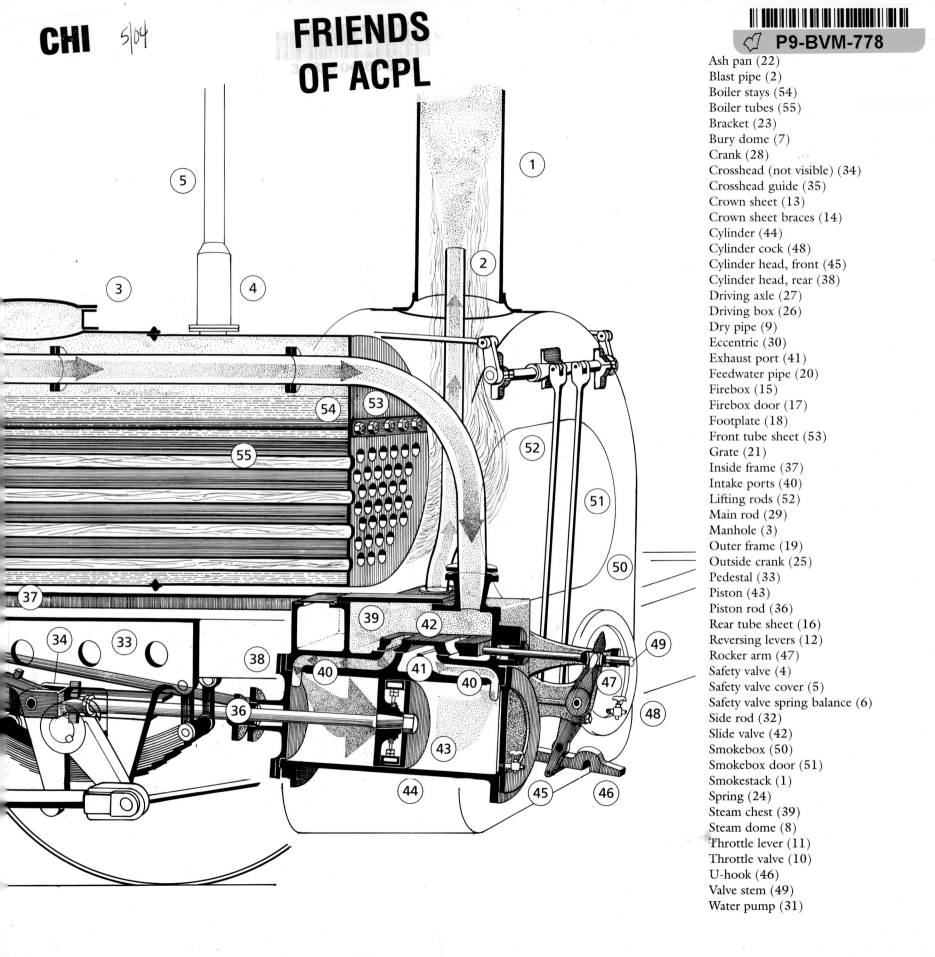

P9-BVM-778

Ash pan (22)
Blast pipe (2)
Boiler stays (54)
Boiler tubes (55)
Bracket (23)
Bury dome (7)
Crank (28)
Crosshead (not visible) (34)
Crosshead guide (35)
Crown sheet (13)
Crown sheet braces (14)
Cylinder (44)
Cylinder cock (48)
Cylinder head, front (45)
Cylinder head, rear (38)
Driving axle (27)
Driving box (26)
Dry pipe (9)
Eccentric (30)
Exhaust port (41)
Feedwater pipe (20)
Firebox (15)
Firebox door (17)
Footplate (18)
Front tube sheet (53)
Grate (21)
Inside frame (37)
Intake ports (40)
Lifting rods (52)
Main rod (29)
Manhole (3)
Outer frame (19)
Outside crank (25)
Pedestal (33)
Piston (43)
Piston rod (36)
Rear tube sheet (16)
Reversing levers (12)
Rocker arm (47)
Safety valve (4)
Safety valve cover (5)
Safety valve spring balance (6)
Side rod (32)
Slide valve (42)
Smokebox (50)
Smokebox door (51)
Smokestack (1)
Spring (24)
Steam chest (39)
Steam dome (8)
Throttle lever (11)
Throttle valve (10)
U-hook (46)
Valve stem (49)
Water pump (31)

THE
# JOHN BULL

For John H. White, Jr.

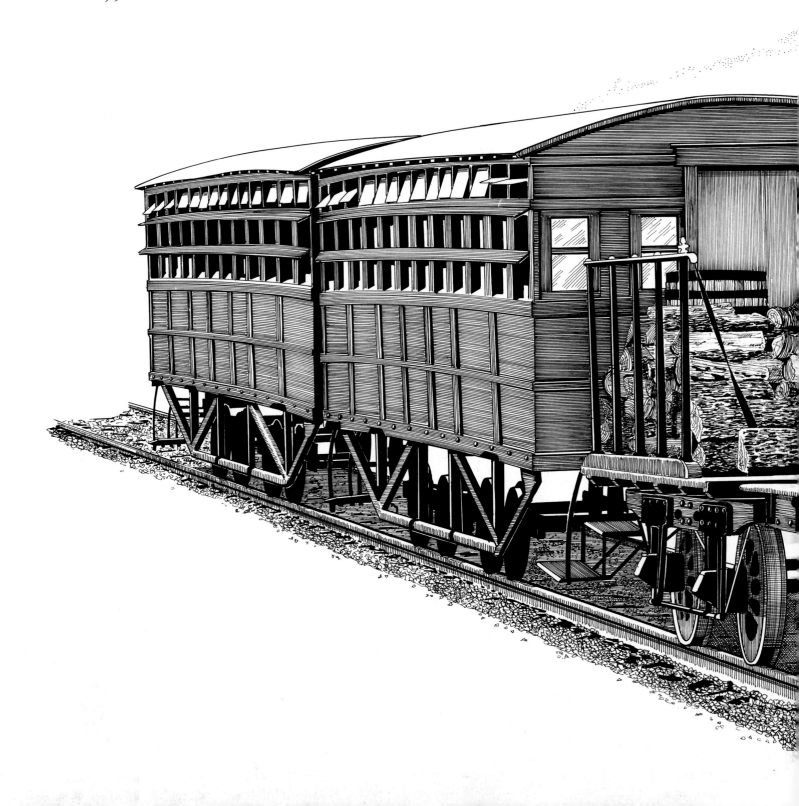

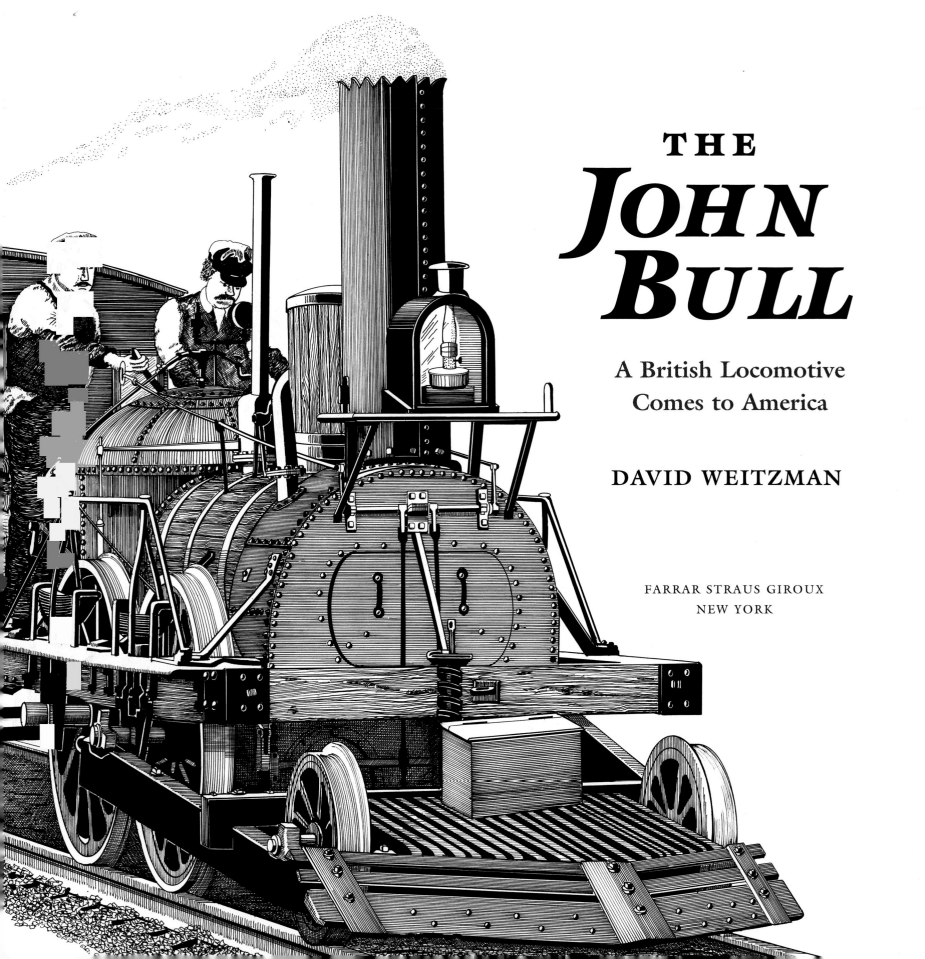

# THE
# JOHN
# BULL

A British Locomotive
Comes to America

## DAVID WEITZMAN

FARRAR STRAUS GIROUX
NEW YORK

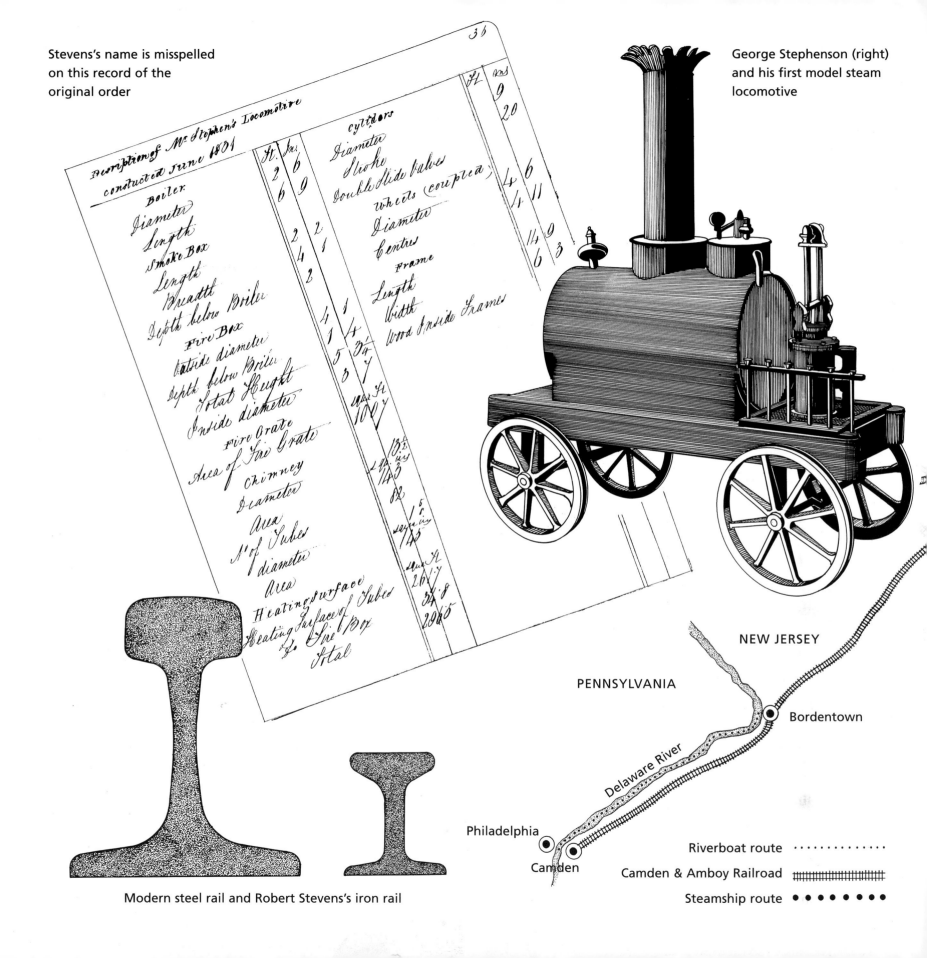

Stevens's name is misspelled on this record of the original order

George Stephenson (right) and his first model steam locomotive

Modern steel rail and Robert Stevens's iron rail

PENNSYLVANIA

NEW JERSEY

Delaware River

Bordentown

Philadelphia

Camden

Riverboat route ·············

Camden & Amboy Railroad ▓▓▓▓▓▓▓▓▓▓

Steamship route ●●●●●●●●●

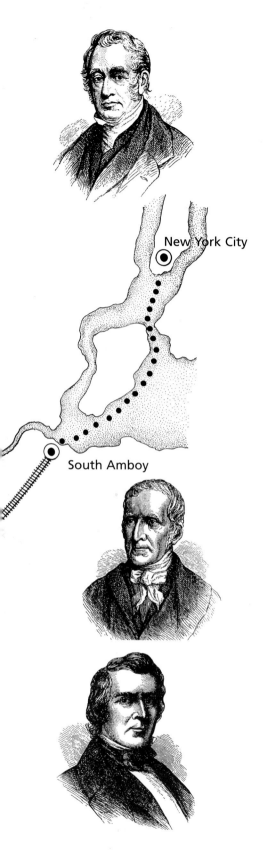

Colonel John Stevens and Robert Stevens, father-and-son railroad builders

**R**obert Stevens is shopping for a steam locomotive. That's not an easy task in America in 1830. Oh, there are a few mechanics tinkering away in shops and barns, and it won't be long before Americans build locomotives. But for now, few Americans have seen or even heard of a steam locomotive, to say nothing of knowing how one works.

Robert grew up with steam power. In 1825, his father, Colonel John Stevens, had made a full-size locomotive that he ran around an oval track on the grounds of their home in Hoboken. That same year the Stevenses received a charter to form the Camden & Amboy Railroad and Transportation Company, connecting Philadelphia and New York, America's two most populous cities.

Americans need better transportation. Factories and farms are producing goods faster than they can be moved. The system of canals and turnpikes was a good start. But canals freeze and roads turn to mud in the winter. Ponderous freight wagons drawn by teams of horses lumber along rutted roads, taking weeks to get anywhere. And the expense! Shipping a bushel of wheat from Buffalo to New York City—about four hundred miles—ends up costing three times its market value.

If the *United* States of America is to become a fact rather than just a dream, then somehow people living in far-flung cities, towns, and farms spread across immense states and territories will have to be brought together. Railroads make that promise.

So Robert Stevens is on his way to Newcastle, England, and the shops of Robert Stephenson and Company. He has a lot of time on the month-long voyage, so he takes out his jackknife and begins whittling on a block of pine provided by the ship's carpenter. What emerges is his design for an iron T-rail that will one day become the world standard.

The history of the steam locomotive began in England in 1804, with Richard Trevithick's marvelous clockwork engine. It must have been quite a sight, all whirring gears, spinning crank and flywheel, belching smoke and sparks from its stack, piston rods shooting back and forth almost six feet. No wonder the first locomotives were called "fiery chariots." But while fun to watch, Trevithick's locomotive was slow—five miles per hour tops—broke down frequently, tore up the cast-iron rails that were too light to carry its weight, and was soon taken out of service.

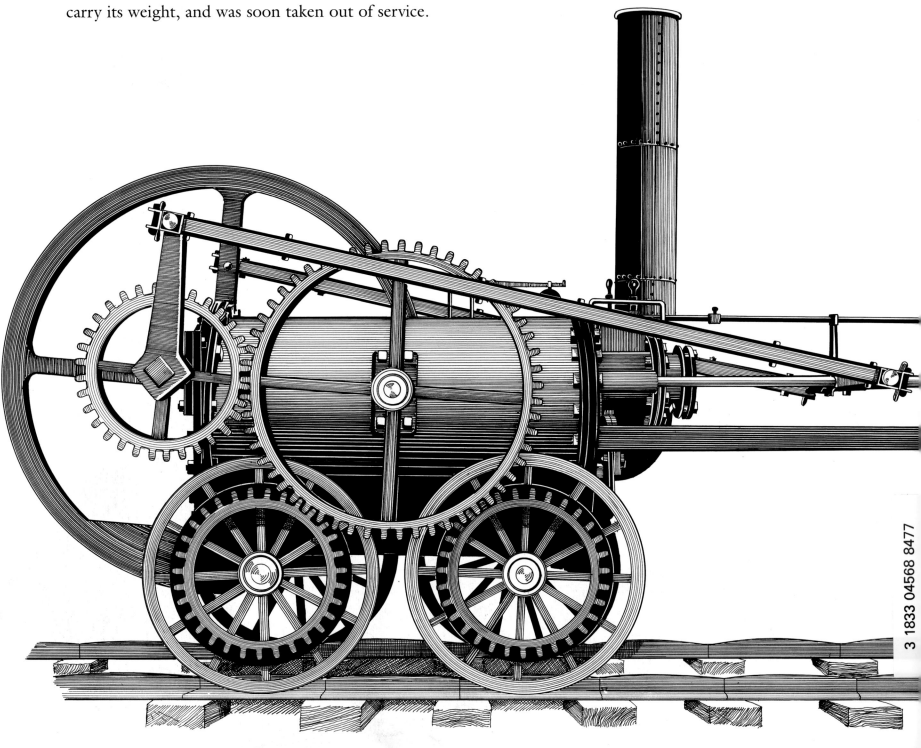

3 1833 04568 8477

The modern locomotive began with the *Rocket*, built by George Stephenson and his son, Robert, who since the age of nineteen had worked with his father on locomotive design and construction, becoming an expert. Not only was the Stephensons' design marvelously simple—instead of all those gears, the pistons drove the wheels directly through connecting rods—but the *Rocket* reached a speed of nearly thirty miles an hour! No one in all of history, up until that time, had ever traveled that fast.

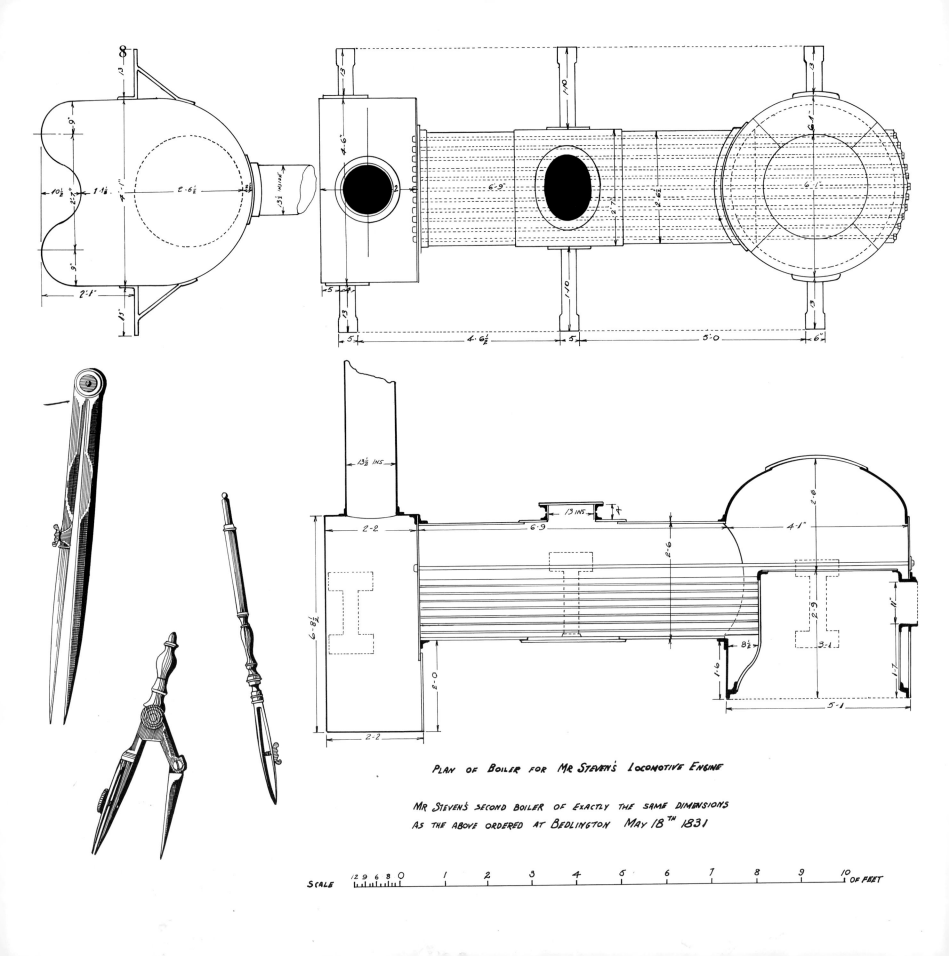

PLAN OF BOILER FOR MR. STEVEN'S LOCOMOTIVE ENGINE

MR. STEVEN'S SECOND BOILER OF EXACTLY THE SAME DIMENSIONS
AS THE ABOVE ORDERED AT BEDLINGTON MAY 18TH 1831

SCALE 12 9 6 8 0     1     2     3     4     5     6     7     8     9     10
OF FEET

By the time Robert Stevens arrives in England, however, Stephenson has already shelved the *Rocket* in favor of an improved design, the *Planet*. The big difference is that the cylinders are placed inside the smokebox—keeping the steam hot—and the pistons and connecting rods drive cranks on the rear axle.

After seeing the *Planet* in service, Stevens decides that's the kind of locomotive he wants. And he has some ideas of his own. He's taken a fancy to the big domed "haystack" firebox he saw on another builder's locomotive, and asks Stephenson to include it in his design. The boiler Stephenson used for the *Rocket* and the *Planet*, called a "wagontop" boiler, is easier to fabricate, but the haystack boiler, Stevens reasons, holds more steam. Besides, while English locomotives burn coal, Stevens's locomotive will burn wood, needing a larger grate area and firebox.

The Stephenson shop was one of the first to prepare drawings for building locomotives. Only one or two general arrangement drawings like this one of the *John Bull*'s boiler are made for each locomotive design. Detailed drawings are sketched out roughly on foolscap paper and then marked out in chalk on the floor of the forge, boiler shop, and machine shop. These simple sketches are all that is needed for the skilled craftsmen to fashion the finished part.

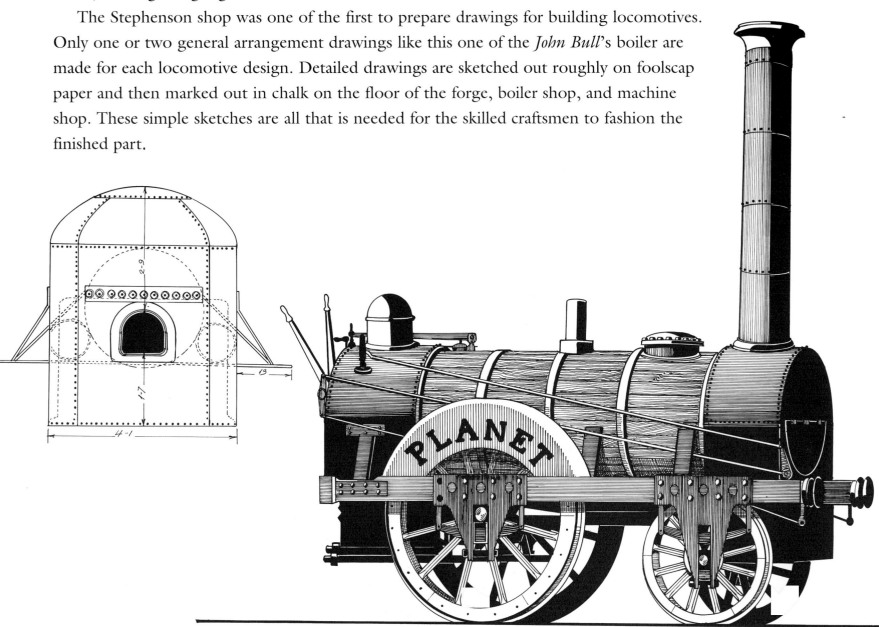

The *John Bull*'s hardworking parts are wrought in the forge. "Hammermen" make all the forgings for locomotives, such as axles, large and small links, motion bars, connecting rods, crossheads, and piston rods. Working iron under the hammer does more than give it shape. The repeated heating and hammering removes impurities and makes the iron more malleable, less brittle, better able to withstand twisting.

Robert Stephenson does not have his own forge. Instead he has his work done at a forge like the one in this drawing.

The hammer is worked by a waterwheel (1) and gears (2) turning the axletree, which is made from the trunk of a huge oak (5). The big gear driving a smaller gear makes the axletree turn much faster than the waterwheel. The momentum of the spinning iron flywheel (3) keeps the machinery running smoothly and steadily. Around the axletree are spaced wooden cams (4) that come down one after the other on the back of the pivoted hammer helve (6), tripping it upward. When the cam releases the helve, the hammer (7) drops with a heavy blow on the anvil (8). The hammer strikes the anvil a ground-shaking, ear-splitting 160 times a minute. It's hard to imagine the noise in a forge with a dozen hammers working at once. The lever (9) enables the hammerman to start and stop the hammer by opening and closing the sluice gate controlling the flow of water to the waterwheel.

An axle begins as pieces of scrap iron piled together (10), heated in a chafery hearth, and then hammered by two workers with sledgehammers into a solid lump, called a loop (11). The loop is returned to the hearth until red-hot and then hammered into an oblong block, or bloom (12). Once again, the bloom returns to the hearth to be hammered into an anchony (13), just the right shape for the hammermen to work into an axle. The cranks, set at a right angle to each other (14), are formed in a U-shaped die set on the anvil.

Most of the locomotive's five thousand parts are made from rolled iron. Instead of being hammered into shapes, the bloom is heated in a hearth to a glowing red and then put through a series of rolls. The first pass is made with the rolls far apart. Gradually, after each pass, the rolls are screwed closer and closer together, squeezing the bloom into a long bar.

The bar is then passed through finishing rolls, to become the round, square, and flat shapes from which the hammermen and blacksmiths create thousands of parts. Round bars are fashioned into rods and bolts. Passed through long, smooth rolls, bars become plates which will be shaped into the *John Bull*'s boiler, firebox, and smokebox. Flat bars (1) are made into rims for the drive wheels, and angle iron (2) becomes the tires.

To become rims and tires, the iron bars, raised to a red heat, are wrapped around a circular mandril, or form. One end of the bar is secured to the mandril by a staple and then bent around with the help of levers and blows of a sledgehammer. Staples dropped over the tire and mandril hold the circular shape until the tire cools. Finally, when the circle is complete, a blacksmith will place the two ends in the hot coals of his forge, get them to a red heat, and hammer them together into a smooth weld.

The *John Bull*'s drive wheels are fashioned of locust wood, in the way wheelwrights have made carriage and wagon wheels for centuries. Wheels are supplied by an old coachmaking firm. The nave (central hub) and felloes (segments of the rim) are mortised to receive the tenons on each end of the spokes. The felloes are put together with dowels. An iron ring, called a "horse collar," is attached to the spokes to make the wheel more rigid.

The inside diameter of the tire is actually a little too small to fit over the wheel. But when heated on a ring of coals, the tire expands, just enough to be driven onto the wooden wheel with sledgehammers. The cooling tire contracts, gripping the wheel with tremendous force. Among the wheelwright's many skills is knowing just how much smaller the tire must be to shrink tightly onto the wheel center.

Another English tradition is coming to America with the *John Bull*: the English gauge. The gauge of English locomotives—the distance between the rails—is the customary spacing of wagon wheels throughout England, 4 feet 8½ inches. In the next few decades railroads in America will be built to more than a dozen different gauges, but the English gauge will eventually prevail, setting the standard for railroads throughout the United States.

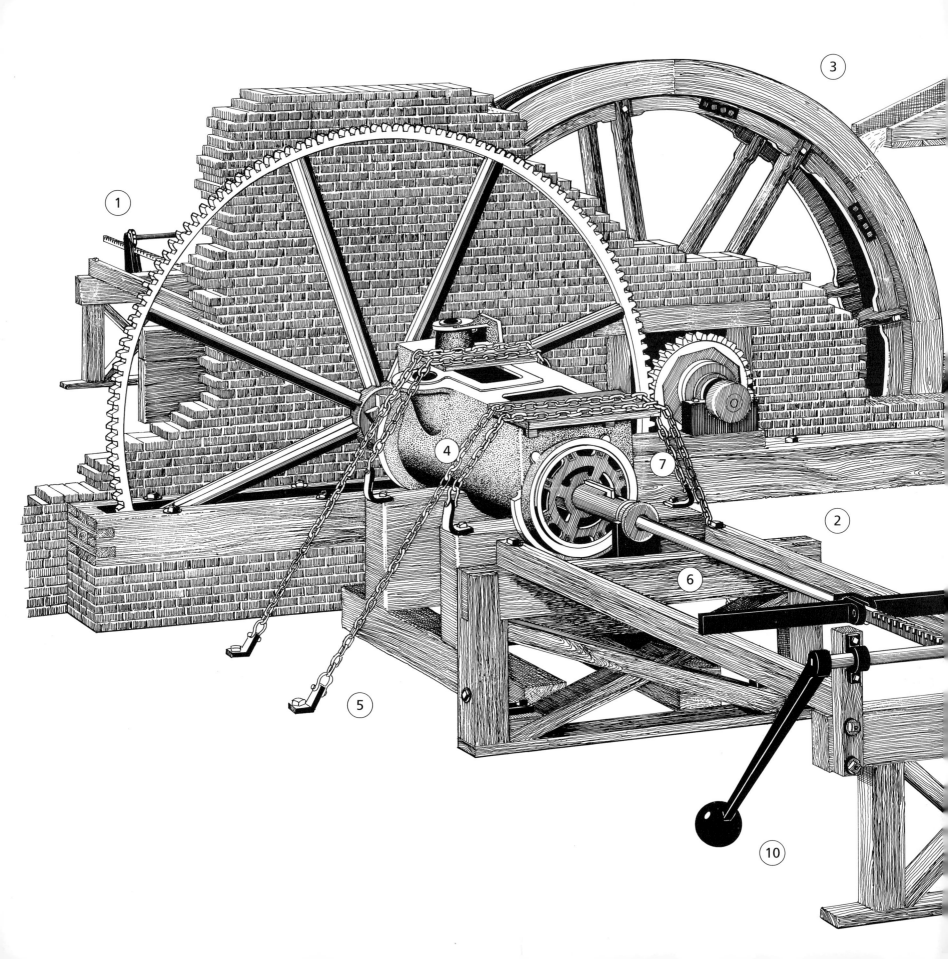

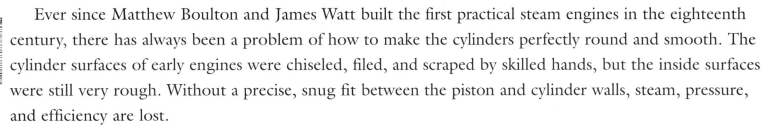

Ever since Matthew Boulton and James Watt built the first practical steam engines in the eighteenth century, there has always been a problem of how to make the cylinders perfectly round and smooth. The cylinder surfaces of early engines were chiseled, filed, and scraped by skilled hands, but the inside surfaces were still very rough. Without a precise, snug fit between the piston and cylinder walls, steam, pressure, and efficiency are lost.

Accurate machining of the cylinders became the most important problem to be solved before an efficient steam locomotive could be built. Then, just a few years before Robert Stephenson began building locomotives, John Wilkinson invented a waterwheel-powered boring mill.

Here the *John Bull*'s two iron cylinders are being bored at one time on two boring mills, back to back (1, 2), run by the same waterwheel (3). One of the *John Bull*'s cylinders (4) can be seen clamped solidly in place with chains (5). A long boring bar (6) is passed through the cylinders and attached to the large gear. This arrangement of a small gear driving a much larger gear makes the boring bar turn very slowly. On the boring bar is mounted a cutterhead (7), positioned at the cylinder opening. The cutting tools are made hard enough to cut iron by repeatedly heating them and then quenching them quickly in water or oil.

Now the machining can begin. The sluice gate is opened, allowing water to fall on the wheel. The boring bar and cutterhead turn slowly. The close end of the boring bar is attached to a rack (8) and pinion (9). When the weighted lever (10) is in the raised position, it falls slowly, turning the pinion and pulling the rack and cutterhead toward us. As the cutterhead spins around, it is pulled through the cylinder from one end to the other, cutting a perfectly round, smooth surface. In the drawing we can see the cutterhead emerging from the cylinder. On the floor behind the millwright are two of the many sizes of cutterheads.

With the machining of the cylinders, the manufacturing work is done. The locomotive is assembled, steamed up, run, and then made ready for its journey to America. On July 14, 1831, "one locomotive steam engine" is loaded aboard the good ship *Allegheny* in the port of Liverpool.

Total cost: £784 7s, or about $4,000.

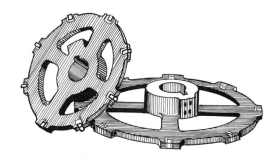

This drawing is called a "section" drawing because the locomotive has been cut through to show a section of the insides. Only the workings on the right, or near, side of the locomotive—cylinder, piston and piston rod, connecting rod, crank, and eccentric—are shown for clarity. In the real locomotive there is another set on the left side.

1. To run the *John Bull*, the boiler is filled with water until the firebox and iron tubes are covered.

2. A blazing fire is built on the grate.

3. Smoke is drawn through the seventy-four iron tubes, into the smokebox, and up the stack.

4. Waves of heat rise from the boiler, pinging and popping as the water reaches boiling and the *John Bull* comes alive.

5. As the water boils, steam pressure builds inside the boiler. Five pounds per square inch. Ten pounds. Fifteen, twenty. Twenty-five. Thirty pounds . . .

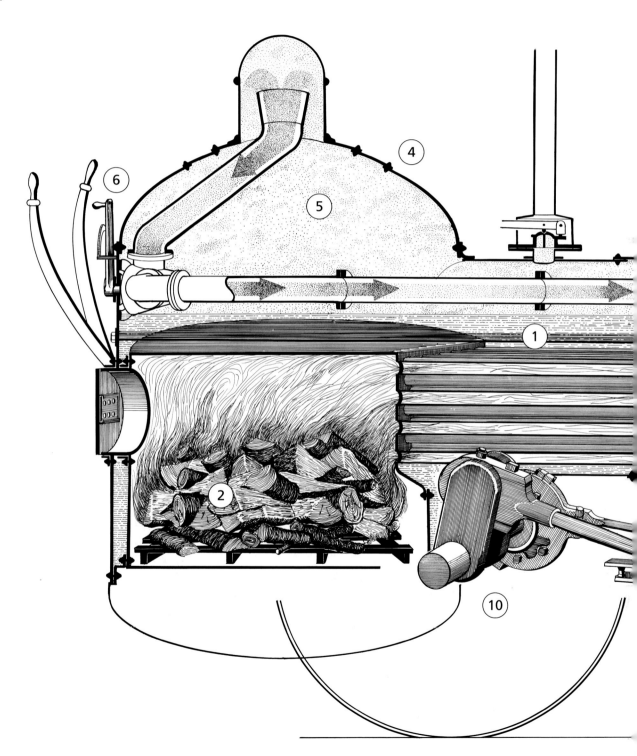

Nor can Isaac ask anyone for help. Stevens is the only one he knows who has even seen a locomotive like this one, and he's away on business. Undaunted, Isaac begins trying the hundreds of pieces to see how they fit together. He marvels at the finely cut threads on the nuts and bolts. Accurate screw-cutting lathes have just recently appeared in England, and in a few years Americans will have them too, but for now the craftsmanship is remarkable. And the cylinders! American foundries have not yet learned to make such complicated iron castings.

Just ten days later, the *John Bull* stands on a short length of track, ready for its test run. Isaac decides the locomotive needs a tender to carry wood and water to make steam. So he finds a four-wheeled flat car and loads it with split wood and a whiskey keg full of water, which he connects to the locomotive with a leather hose made by the local shoemaker.

As soon as Stevens returns, he and Isaac prepare the locomotive for its trial run. It takes some fiddling, adjusting, and even dismantling and reassembling, but soon the *John Bull* is running. Robert and Isaac take turns at the throttle, learning to operate the reversing levers and valve gear as their new locomotive steams up and down the track.

But the *John Bull* will not be put to work just yet. There's to be a celebration and a feast, the guest list to include members of the New Jersey legislature and a French prince, whose wife will become that day—November 12, 1831— the first woman in America to ride as a passenger on a steam-powered train.

The party over, the *John Bull* will spend the next eighteen months in a wooden shed, awaiting the construction of the Camden-to-Amboy line.

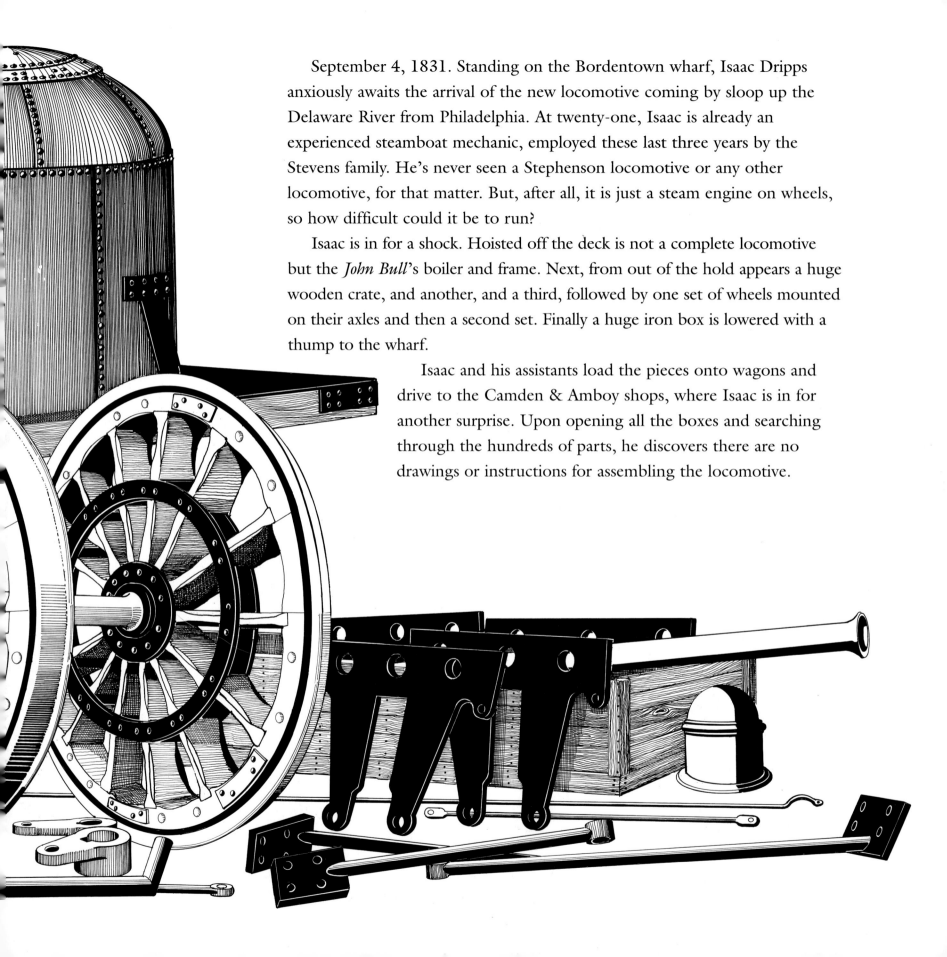

September 4, 1831. Standing on the Bordentown wharf, Isaac Dripps anxiously awaits the arrival of the new locomotive coming by sloop up the Delaware River from Philadelphia. At twenty-one, Isaac is already an experienced steamboat mechanic, employed these last three years by the Stevens family. He's never seen a Stephenson locomotive or any other locomotive, for that matter. But, after all, it is just a steam engine on wheels, so how difficult could it be to run?

Isaac is in for a shock. Hoisted off the deck is not a complete locomotive but the *John Bull*'s boiler and frame. Next, from out of the hold appears a huge wooden crate, and another, and a third, followed by one set of wheels mounted on their axles and then a second set. Finally a huge iron box is lowered with a thump to the wharf.

Isaac and his assistants load the pieces onto wagons and drive to the Camden & Amboy shops, where Isaac is in for another surprise. Upon opening all the boxes and searching through the hundreds of parts, he discovers there are no drawings or instructions for assembling the locomotive.

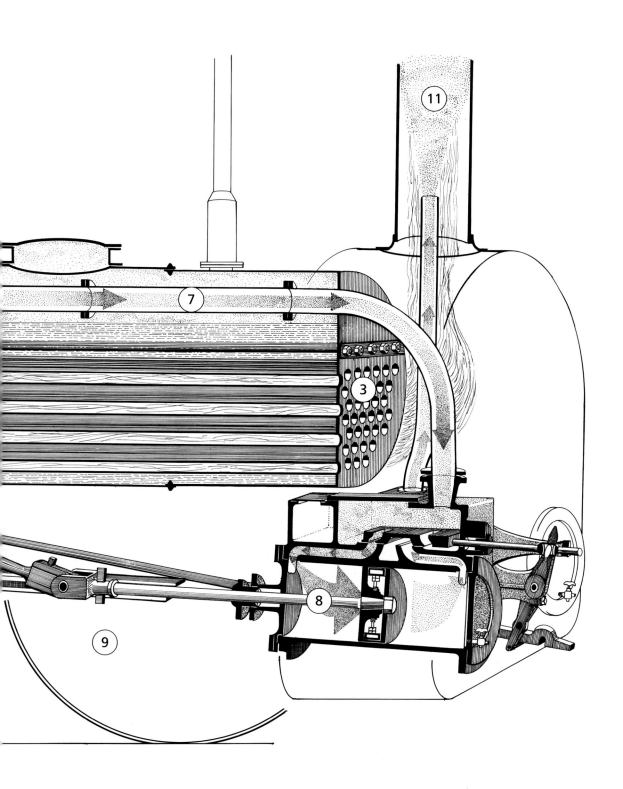

6. The throttle valve is opened.

7. Steam is released from the boiler into the large dry pipes and down into the steam chests.

8. Steam rushes into the cylinders, expanding against the pistons with a force of thousands of pounds.

9. The force moves through the piston rods and connecting rods to the cranks, making the wheels turn.

10. The off-center eccentrics mounted on the axle move the slide valve back and forth so that steam is let first into one side of the cylinder and then into the other.

11. Exhaust steam is let out through the center port of the valve and up a pipe into the stack, making the familiar *chuff-chuff-chuffing* of steam locomotives.

By late 1833, sixty-three miles of track between Amboy and Camden have been laid and the *John Bull* begins regular service. Over the next few years, Isaac and Robert tinker constantly with the locomotive. An oil lamp is placed up front. The *John Bull* is fitted out with cast-iron wheels (the yawing, twisting strokes of the pistons proved too much for the wooden wheels and they soon failed). Improvements are made to the cumbersome reversing gear. A cab is added on to protect the enginemen from the weather, and, most impressive of all, a huge spark-arresting funnel-shaped smokestack is installed to protect forests from the hot cinders. Isaac installs a whistle atop the steam dome to signal the brakeman and train crew, and a bell to announce the coming of the train.

Being able to warn people, animals, and wagons crossing the tracks is important. A collision with a cow or heavily loaded wagon could end up with the locomotive in a ditch, along with the tender and several cars. Since the tracks cross countless roads and paths, run through miles of unfenced pasture, and right through the middle of towns, collisions with livestock and wagons are a constant danger. Isaac's solution is the new cowcatcher, which pushes aside anything on the tracks.

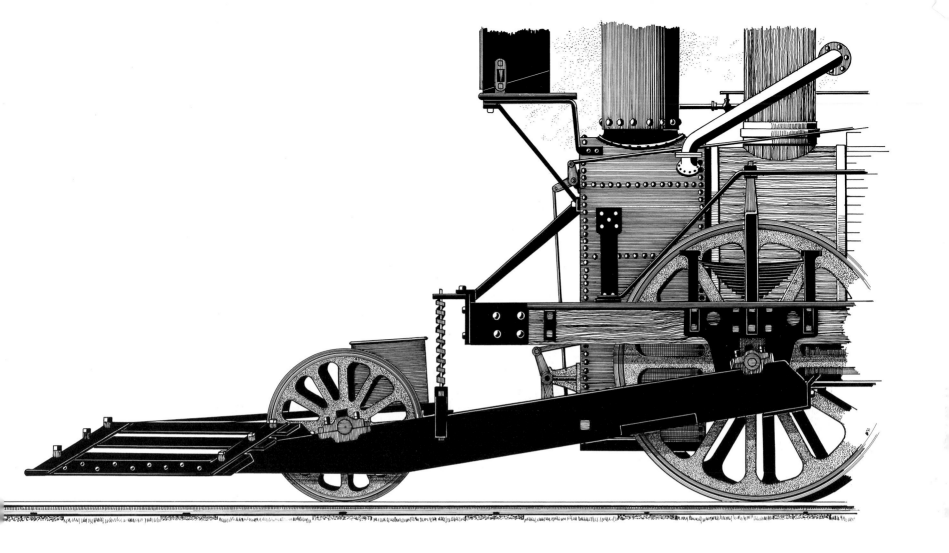

But there's more to the *John Bull*'s cowcatcher. The two small wheels added out in front—called leading, or pilot wheels—are the ingenious answer to a serious problem. The *John Bull* encounters sharper curves in the rugged American countryside than it would in England. When the drive wheels of a fast-moving locomotive come to a sharp turn, the tracks go right or left but the momentum of the heavy locomotive and train is all forward. At high speeds the flange on the first set of drivers hits the inside of the curved rail, climbs over, and sends the locomotive and its train hurtling out into that field of corn.

So Isaac comes up with the idea of pilot wheels. After installing them on the *John Bull*, he walks alongside watching to see what happens as the locomotive enters a sharp curve. Sure enough, he sees the pilot wheels pull the locomotive around into the curve so that the front drive wheel flanges never touch the inside of the rail.

Pilot wheels—two, four, and even six—will guide every passenger and freight locomotive in America for more than a century of steam railroading to come.

The *John Bull* proves to be such a successful design that the Camden & Amboy builds two similar locomotives, buying a few parts, like cylinders, from Stephenson, and ordering thirteen others from American builders. Mechanics gain much experience from all this experimenting with English locomotives and their own designs. At first, locomotives are a sideline of machine shops and manufacturers of textile machinery. But within just a few years after Isaac assembled the *John Bull*, there are some forty manufacturers of locomotives in America.

Americans take to the railroad. The year the *John Bull* arrives, there are twenty-three miles of track in all of America. By 1840, there will be three thousand miles of track. And by 1866, when the little locomotive is at last retired, the country is crisscrossed by forty thousand miles of track—more track than in all the nations of Europe combined. Three years later the first transcontinental railroad is completed, linking the east and west coasts. The trip between New York and Philadelphia, which once took Benjamin Franklin six days, now takes a few hours. In 1833—just two years after the *John Bull*'s arrival—the C&A is carrying over a hundred thousand passengers, often as many as a thousand a day.

Early on, American locomotive builders break with English practices. Instead of placing the cylinders inside the frames and smokebox, driving cranked axles, they bring the cylinders outside to drive the wheels directly. The long distances and steep mountains here call for heavier locomotives with bigger boilers and fireboxes and more drive wheels—six, eight, ten, twelve, eventually sixteen—for enough pulling-power to haul long trains of freight and passenger cars thousands of miles over high mountains.

Eventually, the *John Bull* grows tiny next to more powerful locomotives and is taken out of service. Somehow it is saved from the scrapyard. The Stevens family has grown attached to what has become a curiosity—and, surely, a source of fond memories—keeping it at the Bordentown shops. Every now and then, for world's fairs, expositions, railroad fairs, the United States Centennial, and other celebrations, the little engine is fired up to the delight of new generations.

In 1884, the *John Bull* finds a home away from the hubbub of the rail yards at the Smithsonian Institution in Washington, D.C.—becoming the first engineering artifact in the museum's collection.

And there it sits until 1980, when, to celebrate the locomotive's 150th birthday, curator John H. White, Jr., does more than wonder what it would be like to steam up the old engine again—he decides to do it. But there are so many questions. Are all the parts still there? Will the wheels, pistons, and valves move freely? Is the boiler still sound enough to contain fifty pounds of steam? For several days the curators and technicians check every fitting and pipe connection. The cylinders are still smooth and shiny inside. Everything is tight. The wheels are turned over with a pry bar to make sure none of the moving parts is jammed. The whistle on the steam dome is removed and an air hose attached. White explains what happens next.

"I intended to conduct only a leak test that day, but the jacks and timbers were already in place and the rear wheels could be lifted from the rails with just a few clicks of the ratchets. Why not? The day before, they had doused all the bearings and running surfaces with oil. The pressure built up to forty pounds, the safety valve began to rattle, and so I tugged at the throttle. Air surged down the dry pipe, through the valve ports, and into the cylinders. An instant later the old fossil roared back to life. With a hoarse bark a great cloud of dust erupted out of the stack, the accumulation of nearly half a century. After a few more husky snorts, the *John Bull* settled down to a quiet ticking sound, no louder than a well-oiled steeple clock."

Running the *John Bull* on live steam is another question. A team from the Hartford Steam Boiler Inspection and Insurance Company radiographs the boilerplate and seams to check for any hidden cracks. Just like at the dentist's office, film is taped to the inside of the boiler and exposed to X-rays. The boilerplate appears sound. Ultrasonic tests come up with no hidden defects in the cranks, rods, or cylinder walls. Next comes a hydrostatic test—filling the boiler with water and then raising the pressure to fifty pounds to find the leaks. Water sprays everywhere, but soon all is tight as can be. The *John Bull* has passed all the tests and is now ready to run.

The locomotive is placed in a wooden crib on heavy rollers, rolled across the marble floors of the museum to the freight elevator, lowered to the basement loading dock, lifted onto a flatbed truck, and, under the autumn sun, carried to the Southern Railway tracks near Calverton, Virginia.

Over the next few days, the Smithsonian crew learns the secrets of operating the locomotive much as Isaac and Robert must have done. "None of us was certain what might happen—we weren't really too sure about how the valve gear worked." It turns out to be more than a wonderful thing to do. "In the course of firing up and operating the engine," Jack White writes later, "we gained several fresh and important insights into the history and design of the locomotive . . . which could only have come from the actual hands-on experience."

September 11, 1981, one hundred and fifty years to the day after John Stevens and Isaac Dripps first ran the *John Bull*. Dignitaries, the TV and press corps, and hundreds wait. The Marine Corps Band strikes up a fanfare. Drums roll, and John White tugs on the throttle. Nothing. The little locomotive which had done so well through all of its tests has become cantankerous. An hour later, after the sticky throttle was unstuck and almost everyone had gone home, the *John Bull* chuffs up and down the Georgetown branch, just as smoothly as you please.

The *John Bull* remains on exhibit at the National Museum of American History in Washington, D.C.

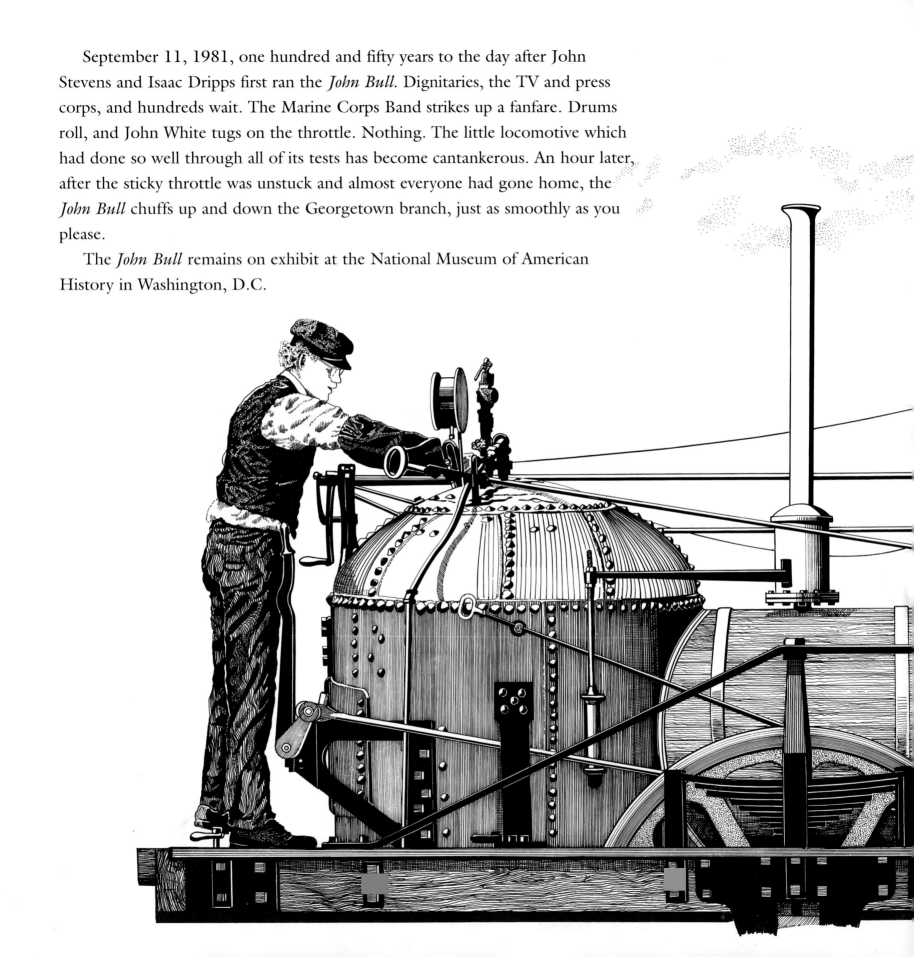

Acknowledgments

This story required the help of many people and two exciting journeys. Richard Gibbon and Sarah Norville organized my visit to the National Railway Museum in York, England, and put me in the charge of Rodney Lytton, who introduced me to the *Rocket*—indeed, let me climb all around and touch it—as a way of explaining the work of early locomotive building. Librarian Lynne Thurston had piles of books awaiting me, including the work of Michael Bailey, who then answered my queries over the months of writing with detailed accounts of the Stephenson shop.

At the National Museum of American History, Steve Lubar gave me access to the collections, libraries, the curatorial staff, and the *John Bull*. It was as easy as a knock at an open door. Steve, Bill Worthington, Peter Liebhold, and Robert Vogel talked to me about the shop culture of 1830s England. Bill Withuhn and Larry Jones shared their personal stories of preparing and steaming up the *John Bull*. Susan Tolbert guided me through the photo archives. Claudia Kidwell showed me how to dress the workers in my drawings. Maya Hambly and Peggy Kidwell found measuring and drafting instruments of the period.

Home again, I needed a couple more pieces of the puzzle, which came to me from Kurt Bell at the Railroad Museum of Pennsylvania and Sarah Bennett of the Albany Institute of History and Art.

This book was possible because of John H. White, Jr. There are his many books and articles on the *John Bull* and locomotive history, to be sure, but there is also Jack, who was never too busy to answer my questions during our lengthy, almost weekly telephone calls, responding with sketches, drawings, and thoughtful critiques of my work. He is at the heart of this book, but must not be held responsible for my flights of fancy.

Finally, Nancy Ellis got my *John Bull* proposal to Wesley Adams, who enjoyed and appreciated the story before it was even written.

Copyright © 2004 by David Weitzman
All rights reserved
Distributed in Canada by Douglas & McIntyre Ltd.
Printed and bound in the United States of America by Berryville Graphics
Designed by Nancy Goldenberg
First edition, 2004
1 3 5 7 9 10 8 6 4 2

www.fsgkidsbooks.com

Library of Congress Cataloging-in-Publication Data
Weitzman, David.
    The John Bull : a British locomotive comes to America / David Weitzman.
        p.   cm.
    Summary: Describes how John Bull, a steam locomotive, was built in England, brought
to the United States in 1831, assembled, put to work, and modified over time, leading the
way for modern rail transportation.
    ISBN 0-374-38037-6
    1. John Bull (Steam locomotive)—History—Juvenile literature.   2. Locomotives—Great
Britain—Juvenile literature.   3. Railroads—United States—Juvenile literature.   [1. John Bull
(Steam locomotive).   2. Locomotives—History.   3. Railroads—Trains—History.]   I. Title.
TJ603.4.G7 W45 2004
625.26'1—dc21
                                                                                2003044873

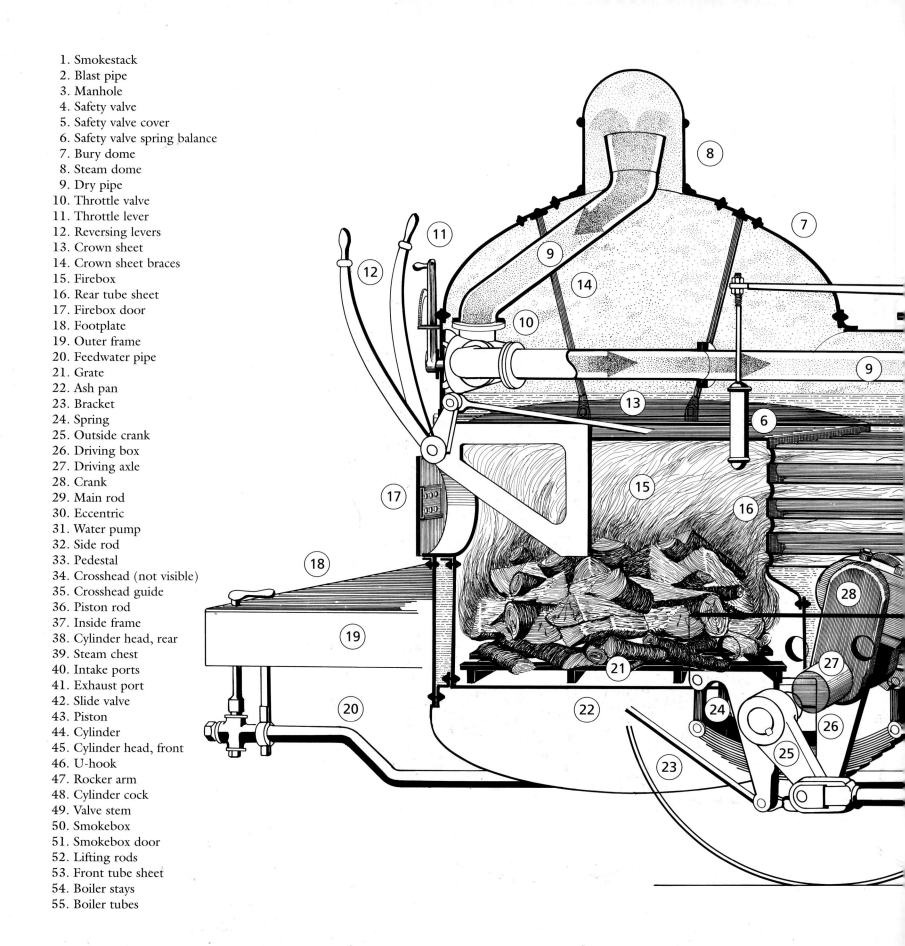

1. Smokestack
2. Blast pipe
3. Manhole
4. Safety valve
5. Safety valve cover
6. Safety valve spring balance
7. Bury dome
8. Steam dome
9. Dry pipe
10. Throttle valve
11. Throttle lever
12. Reversing levers
13. Crown sheet
14. Crown sheet braces
15. Firebox
16. Rear tube sheet
17. Firebox door
18. Footplate
19. Outer frame
20. Feedwater pipe
21. Grate
22. Ash pan
23. Bracket
24. Spring
25. Outside crank
26. Driving box
27. Driving axle
28. Crank
29. Main rod
30. Eccentric
31. Water pump
32. Side rod
33. Pedestal
34. Crosshead (not visible)
35. Crosshead guide
36. Piston rod
37. Inside frame
38. Cylinder head, rear
39. Steam chest
40. Intake ports
41. Exhaust port
42. Slide valve
43. Piston
44. Cylinder
45. Cylinder head, front
46. U-hook
47. Rocker arm
48. Cylinder cock
49. Valve stem
50. Smokebox
51. Smokebox door
52. Lifting rods
53. Front tube sheet
54. Boiler stays
55. Boiler tubes